The Ron Van Clief WHITE BELT GUIDEBOOK

Also by Ron Van Clief

The Manual of the Martial Arts

The Ron Van Clief Green and Purple Belt Guidebook

The RonVan Clief WHITE BELT GUIDEBOOK

Ron Van Clief
Five Times World Champion
in Kung Fu and Karate

SOUVENIR PRESS

Photographs by Bert Torchia, Bill Peck, and Ron Van Clief
Illustrations by Neal Adams, Ken Morais, Dorria Ameen, and Ron Van Clief
Grateful acknowledgment is given to the following for the use of movie stills and nostalgia photos:

Aquarius Films	Mr. Terry Levene
Madison World Films	Mr. Serafim Karalexis
Seasonal Films	Mr. Roy Horan
Filmark Films	Mr. Tomas Tang
Silverstein Films	Mr. Sam Silverstein
Black Dragon Films	Mr. Ron Van Clief

Assistants' credits:
Radu Teodorescu, Marcus Feuerstein, Brian Glatt, Alfred Ng, Libra Lederer, Janet E. Bloem, Don Kennard, Glen Perry, Mike Angelone, William Diaz, Maurice J. Miller, Roscoe Born, Beverly Stowe, Ron Van Clief, Jr., Christopher Wade, Chaka Zulo, Victor Vega, Stephanie Vega, Taimak Guarriello, and Larry Klein
Special thanks to Al Weiss, Alan Vasquez, Herman Petras, and Paul Maslak— *Official Karate and Warriors Magazine*

Published by arrangement with Crown Publishers Inc.

First published in the U.S.A. by
Crown Publishers Inc., New York

First British Edition published 1985 by
Souvenir Press Ltd., 43 Great Russell Street London WC1B 3PA

ISBN 0 285 62697 3

Reproduced from the original American edition,
and printed in Great Britain by
Photobooks (Bristol) Limited

CONTENTS

The 'Everlast' shields and 'Heavy Hands' equipment mentioned in this book refer to American brand names not on sale in Britain. Similar striking pads and light, hand-held weights for punch practice are, however, available, and you should consult your local dealer as to your requirements.

The
RonVan Clief
WHITE BELT
GUIDEBOOK

I
INTRODUCTION TO THE RON VAN CLIEF SYSTEM

The Ron Van Clief System is a complete synthesis of the practical and tactical psychophysical mechanisms. A style is as good as its practitioner and the technology used. First you must develop the proper mental attitude. Then you must build your body to your own specifications. Your style *must acknowledge all your structural limitations*. You achieve new levels of mental and physical awareness through proper martial arts education. Self-defense is only a byproduct. Systematic logic and creative imagination are the foundations of my system. There is no perfect style. There are only workable techniques and unworkable techniques.

People come to the martial arts for different reasons. Most come for either self-defense or mental fitness. Mental fitness occurs when the biocomputer (mind), the compressor (heart and lungs), and the suspension system (legs, trunk) are tuned up.

Martial arts education is not just learning to kick and punch. It teaches you to live your life in peace and harmony. Violence has become a way of life in modern societies. The threat of violence builds a tension within us that changes our behavior. We adapt to society. The study of martial arts enables one to relax and think at all times.

Mental and physical fitness are the two main goals of the study of the martial arts. Fitness is maintenance for the mind! Your mind and your body are one and the same. The Ron Van Clief System is a total mental, spiritual, and physical experience. To progress, you must know your limitations. My style is an expressive outlet. The mental calmness developed by practice allows free self-expression.

My life has changed a great deal during the past thirty years of study. Martial arts have become my way of life. I started my martial arts study in the mid-1950s in Brooklyn, New York. My first teacher was a Chinese man who had a laundry near where I lived. He taught me a style called shaolin boxing (Medieval Chinese kung fu). I had always been an exercise addict as a youth. Sifu taught me in the back of his laundry. (*Sifu* is a Cantonese term meaning teacher.) I would practice my forms, kicks, and punches every day. As a youth I bought every book available on the arts of self-defense. Most books at that time were by Bruce Tegner and there were a few judo and shotokan (second largest karate system in Japan) textbooks. I didn't become interested in competition for another ten years. Competition was something I acquired a taste for in my mid-twenties. My competition phase lasted for over two decades. I competed in judo, karate, and kung fu tournaments. Competition was very exciting for me. It was a way that I could express my technical superiority. Winning was only part of the motivation. I learned a great deal from the matches that I lost. Losing is part of winning. I took pride in being a technician. My family was very supportive toward my training. My mother had motivated me to start body building because I was a skinny kid. My dad taught me boxing when I was about seven years old. I didn't like boxing. It seemed to be very limited in its techniques. Because I used mainly my hands, it seemed as though I wasn't using my body to its fullest potential. I found the martial arts to be the best exercise for the body, mind, and spirit. The martial arts have grown from an obscure discipline to a national sport in only three decades. Self-actualization is the only self-defense mechanism that we have at our disposal. People make things happen! People are not the system; they only create the system. Only motivated people will excel in any endeavor. I have coined a word for highly motivated people who seemingly exceed all known limits: *supernormal. Supernormal* is a term that defines the chosen few, those who go that extra mile. Men and women who go far beyond human scope! These supernormal people have a driving desire to reach their full potential.

Everyone has a self-image, and this self-image forms our personalities and behavior patterns. The mainstay of the Ron Van Clief System is to teach you how to feel good about yourself. The Ron Van Clief System is 90 percent mental and 10 percent physical. A proper mental attitude is the most important overall development.

Our bodies change with age. It is false to think that we will always have our physical prowess as we age. Wisdom is the ability to decipher life's trials and experiences and determine the true meaning of perception. How we perceive our lives determines how we will deal with the people who enter our space and time. I have always believed in physical fitness. Because of the martial arts, I now realize the importance of mental fitness. Mental fitness determines our spiritual and physical consciousness.

My form of training enables you to express yourself with individual techniques. Your choice of techniques is limited only by your mind's flexibility. There are more than five thousand techniques in the Ron Van Clief System. Because of the vast number of techniques available, you can use only what feels comfortable to you. Most styles are too structured to be realistic. Also, everyone is different structurally and mentally. The style that you choose to study must be adapted to your own body.

The Americanization of the martial arts was just a matter of time. America has always been the land of innovation and invention. American martial arts is a totally new concept devised by many pioneers, such as Peter Urban, Ed Parker, Bruce Lee, and Chuck Norris. The martial arts have replaced the old westerns and action films. Kung fu movies are on all the satellite and cable television networks. I think that the martial arts will become the most popular sport in America! The martial arts will be taught in the schools of our nation, as in the Orient. I believe that the practice of martial arts explains why the Oriental has become such a fierce competitor in the world market. Due to the abilities of intense concentration and discipline that they gain, work habits become normal habits. The ability to express our full potential is necessary for total individual development throughout our lives.

In the past three decades I have had the honor of seeing some of the greatest masters of the arts in the world. I would like to share my experiences and knowledge with you. Understanding oneself is the first priority of study. Knowing your weak and strong points is crucial to realistic evaluation. Your framework of reality should be based on objective analysis and systematic logic. Grandmaster Peter Urban taught me more than anyone else in the field of Zen. Sensei is a Zen master. His teachings have allowed me to see myself in Zen terms. Zen is different for everyone! Plan your work, work your plan . . . because organization is self-learning. Set your priorities and go for them! Good luck in your studies, and may the force of the true martial arts spirit be with you forever. In the next chapter we will discuss the White Belt workout. Remember, the process of self-learning never stops!

Hwang Jang Lee, *Invincible Armor*

Kung fu is more than four thousand years old. Chinese, Japanese, African, and European roots form what we know today as martial arts. I have been involved in the various martial arts for three decades. My studies range from traditional forms of China and Japan to the hybrid styles of America. American martial artists are the overall best in the area of sparring and weapons. We can learn much about the classic styles from the old masters. Mental and spiritual development maximizes the effect of your training. The proper attitude is to totally commit yourself to the task at hand. You must maintain a stable character to avoid unstable reactions. My mentor, Grandmaster Peter Urban, said, "Keep the good, discard the bad!" Simply, give up bad habits and acquire good ones.

Kurata, *Legend of a Fighter*

Which is better—kung fu or karate? It is not the art that is better or worse. It is the artist. A kung fu punch in the face will hurt as much as a karate punch. I truly believe there is no superior art, but superior martial artists. Kung fu does not abuse your body as much as karate does. You can practice a soft style much longer than a hard style. Karate is too rigid. It shocks the body. Kung fu is much more flexible, as a rule. A combination of kung fu and karate is optimum.

Hong Kong, 1974. This shot was taken after a workout at the Wing Tsun headquarters. To my left is Grandmaster Leung Ting; next to him is Grandmaster Charles Bonet. Leung Ting was Bruce Lee's older gung fu brother.

Sue Shiomi, *Dragon Princess*

Women in the martial arts! Sportswomen are a fascinating breed of animal—they're supernormal. I have seen some great women in the martial arts. They traditionally excel in kata (the dictionary of martial arts) and form. Most women are much more stretched out than their male counterparts. My first real karate teacher was a woman. She taught me about Okinawan karate. Okinawa is said to be the origin of the major karate disciplines in Japan and China. In the past three decades, I have taught hundreds of women worldwide.

Jacky Chan and Simon Yuen, *Snake in the Eagle's Shadow*

Jacky Chan has become an international kung fu superstar. He has become a living legend, as did Bruce Lee. It takes a lot of hard work and energy to make it in any field. Jacky combines humor with splendid acrobatic prowess. Gymnastics make the films more fantastic and, therefore, entertaining. Jacky's films have made millions of dollars. Jacky got his big start in films at Seasonal Films in Hong Kong. He was developed by Ng See Yuen into an international superstar. There have been comparisons made between Jacky and Bruce Lee. They have two completely different, distinct styles of expression. Jacky's comic attitude adds flavor to the kung fu fighting sequences. Bruce was the Clint Eastwood of the martial arts. There will always be new superstars, but none will ever replace Bruce Lee.

Unicorn Chan, little brother to Bruce Lee. Unicorn Chan was a good friend to Bruce Lee. Leo Fong introduced me to Unicorn Chan in Manila. I was on location filming *The Bamboo Trap*. Leo Fong produced this film on a shoe string budget. The martial arts were great; the screenplay left something to be desired. Mr. Chan is married to a Philippina and lives in Cebu City. He is quite a martial artist and film director. Although I haven't seen him since 1974, I am sure he is still practicing the martial arts.

Ron Van Clief, *Kung Fu Fever*

What is better—hands or feet? Kicks are used to get close enough to use hand techniques. Kicking is a long-range attack. Punching is for short-range attack. I believe there should be an almost even balance between hand and leg techniques. It is very hard to maintain good strong kicking devices at advanced ages. Some styles overemphasize kicking. It would be very hard to kick somebody in a telephone booth! Korean arts are known for their fancy methods of kicking. A beautiful kick is a beautiful kick! Hand techniques are easier to perform in self-defense situations. Good kicking takes lots of hard work!

Ron Van Clief and Dragon Lee, *Kung Fu Fever*

Kung Fu Fever was one of my most exciting projects. Chinese film-making differs from American standards. First of all, I have never been on a Chinese film that shot with sound. Every company in Asia that makes kung fu movies uses one camera. All the sequences are done over and over again for the different camera angles. Sometimes they have a high-speed camera for the slow-motion effect. High-speed cameras eat up film, so they are used only for special shots. An interesting point about kung fu films with Americans as co-stars is that they are shot with two endings—one ending for the Asian market, another for the European. The Asians don't buy tickets to see a foreign star. The American audiences are still under the misconception that only Orientals can do martial arts. If you learn the correct techniques, with the proper attitude, progress is guaranteed. Chuck Norris has proved that Americans can be successful at action film-making. His last few films have grossed more than some of the Bruce Lee films. Chuck Norris is an American kung fu superstar of the highest order.

The Death of Bruce Lee

This film, *The Death of Bruce Lee*, is my favorite. It was my second starring role, and it was the first opportunity that I had to express my artistic ability. Being one of the action directors on a Chinese film was an honor. Normally, foreigners follow an Oriental martial arts choreographer. I developed a rapport with the director and producer. You must be creative in filmland. Everyone can kick and punch. It is how you approach these different fight scenes that makes the difference. It looks as though the actors and stuntmen are getting killed, but they're not! The stuntmen make the stars look good.

I look on martial arts choreography as an art form in itself. It is quite a challenge to make fantasy look real. The Chinese have the best-choreographed action sequences that I have ever seen, especially the shaolin films coming out of mainland China. I learned a great deal about filmmaking from the Chinese. They are craftsmen of their art. The cameraman was called sifu. *Sifu* is a Cantonese word to describe someone that has talent. A good cameraman has accomplished a proficiency with his camera, which qualifies him as a sifu.

2

THE RON VAN CLIEF WHITE BELT WORKOUT

MAINTAINING THE LIFE-SUPPORT SYSTEMS

Health and fitness should be utmost on our priorities for survival. We are what we ingest! Our environment is polluted. Our air and food are full of chemical wastes. Preservatives and additives affect our personalities. Hypertension and heart disease cause more deaths per year than car accidents. As modern people, we must learn to survive these obstacles. The first step is to get in good physical shape. Exercise is necessary for our minds and bodies. It is a medical fact that exercise relieves the effects of stress. Watch what you eat, and start a gradual fitness program. Martial arts is the perfect exercise!

We must first understand that stress is normal. There is good stress and bad stress. The problem is to find the optimum stress level.

Let me explain good stress. Stress equals motivation. Good stress motivates us to acquire our goals; for example, education prepares for the future. College students are under a great deal of stress. Their final goal is to graduate and find a job making good money. Professionals get paid more than unskilled laborers. Good stress helps to develop our finer qualities. Winning is a form of release and total self-expression. Bad stress has the opposite effect. Our normal behavior patterns disintegrate when we are under bad stress. This is sometimes called "Couldn't Cope Syndrome." We tend to withdraw when confronted with bad stress. Bad stress depresses, whereas good stress motivates. Coping is dealing with stress.

Martial arts education enables the student to use the basic philosophies to exist in modern-day society. Learning how to protect yourself is only a byproduct of the martial arts. Mental understanding and physical expression are vehicles through which we develop our total potential. Yogi Zen monks used meditation to achieve a state of physical and spiritual unity for relaxation. We must learn how to relax! Only when we relax are we capable of really using our great untapped mental and physical resources. Stress is either too much or too little! Being properly tuned up is the optimum stress level. Psychophysical drills develop the mind and the body to work together in unison. This chapter discusses some of my favorite exercises.

As human beings we all have basically the same equipment: heart, lungs, kidneys, and other organs necessary for life support. Some people take better care of their cars than their bodies. Our bodies are delicate machines that need daily maintenance. Our food is our fuel. Our legs are our suspension system. Our hearts and lungs are our compressors. The brain, which is the biocomputer, controls all of the body's logic and behavioral programming. Our brains function just as efficiently as microcomputers. The brain is capable of storing vast amounts of data. How we think and what we eat affect our personality. Our life-support systems are a combination of three basic mechanisms: the biocomputer, the compressor, and the suspension system. We must take care of our bodies. Exercise and nutrition are necessary to maintain the proper balance between the biocomputer and the other two systems. We are what we think we are! We are all conditioned by the forces that be. Our environment conditions us to live and think the way we do.

In the past three decades, I have tried many different forms of physical conditioning. Some worked, some didn't. In this chapter, I hope to give you a basic idea of how to get your body into shape. There are two different kinds of shape: competition shape and maintenance shape. Most of us are not even interested in putting in the time necessary to compete. I competed for more than twenty years in various events, ranging from kata (empty hand and with weapons) to sparring, full contact, and noncontact. At some point in competition, the body says, "Is this really worth it?" There isn't any athlete, alive or dead, who never felt that way. After you reach the level where you have mastered your art form, there is competition. I grew bored with competition! My basic belief is that the martial arts are the very best form of exercise for the body and the mind. Competition is another thing. I don't discourage competition or encourage it. But maintenance shape is what I consider the more important of the two types of shape. After years of trying to maintain peak shape, I know it is impossible to be in peak shape forever. Therefore, try not to abuse your body with too much exercise. Your body needs a certain amount of exercise to run properly. More means you wear out the joints and ball bearings. Competition shape burns out the body much quicker than maintenance shape. Progressive resistance must become part of getting into shape for tournaments. Weight training is the most physically demanding form of physical fitness doctrines. In the mid-1950s, I was introduced to the art of body building by Mr. Kenny Hall. Body building and the martial arts were my two hobbies. Shotokan karate and jujitsu were my first two forms of the martial arts education. From the time I was a teenager, my path of learning went from Brooklyn to Okinawa. On Okinawa I studied various forms of karate-do. Each style has a completely different set of warm-up exercises. In this chapter, I will introduce you to my favorite warm-up and maintenance workout. Relax and take control of your minds and bodies!

THE RON VAN CLIEF WHITE BELT WORKOUT

WARM-UP

Jump rope	10 to 20 minutes optimum
Front stretch	10 to 20 reps
Sit-ups/leg raises	10 to 20 reps
The crab	10 to 20 reps
Push-ups	10 to 50 reps optimum

CLOSE-RANGE WEAPONS

Sunfist punch	20 to 100 reps
Corkscrew punch	20 to 50 reps
Snakefist/spearhand	20 to 100 reps
Backfist strike	20 to 100 reps

LONG-RANGE WEAPONS

Front kick	10 to 20 reps
Crescent kick	10 to 15 reps
Reverse crescent kick	10 to 15 reps
Back kick	10 to 15 reps
Round kick	10 to 20 reps
Side kick	10 to 20 reps

PSYCHOPHYSICAL DRILLS

Front kick, backfist, triple sunfist, and reverse chop

Reverse crescent kick, crescent kick, and reverse chop

Snakefist, front kick, crescent kick, reverse crescent kick, and backfist

Front kick, round kick, reverse crescent kick, and triple sunfist

Front kick, round kick, side kick, reverse crescent kick, and crescent kick

All psychophysical drills require the use of all extremities for optimum results. Kicks should allow you to open up with hand techniques. Footwork and balance allow free expression of techniques in delivery. These drills start in the standard shoulder-width stance with the hands in the guard position. It does not matter if you use the primary or secondary limbs for execution. The primary weapon is the limb closest to your target. The secondary weapon is the limb farthest from the target. Practice your drills with both the left and right sides. I practice my techniques first in slow motion, then fluid speed, and finally full speed. These drills require a lot of practice for proficiency. Let the techniques flow from your mind and your body will follow. My karate mentor, Grandmaster Peter Urban, once told me, "Reality is a positive attitude." It was the support of Grandmaster Urban that helped me to develop in the martial arts.

The warm-up is the most important part of the workout. You must get a good supply of blood and oxygen to the muscles. The warm-up prepares the muscles for the job of work. The ideal warm-up lasts about 15 minutes; more is not necessary. Before starting this or any martial arts program, you should get a physical from your doctor. It always pays to be safe! All you need to work out is a loose-fitting garment, sneakers, and a positive mental attitude.

Jumping rope is a great way to start a workout. It is an excellent aerobic exercise. Aerobic exercise promotes better heart and lung efficiency. Aerobic exercise is any rhythmic activity that promotes a sustained increase in heart rate, respiration, and muscle metabolism. The Ron Van Clief System is one of the only systems today that teach aerobic self-defense. Aerobic self-defense is the combination of martial arts techniques with basic aerobic exercise principles. It is best to warm up with some nice music in the background. I use disco and reggae music to back up the pace and timing, but it is up to you what music is used for your workout. The golden rule is to use what makes you feel comfortable.

Front stretch: Stretching the leg muscles and tendons increases flexibility. Relax! Place your palms just above your knee for balance and support. Do not rock or bounce on the leg, which could cause injury. Light, constant pressure is all that is necessary.

Assisted stretch: This is an excellent stretch to develop flexibility. A certain amount of flexibility is necessary to execute leg mechanisms. Make sure that your support leg is bent for stability and balance.

Front split: This is one of the hardest stretches for me to do. You should do this one only when you develop the other stretches. This stretch is not mandatory!

The abdominal segment of this warm-up is my favorite. Always try to include a variety of stomach exercises in your workout. Your stomach is the source of your energy—the gas tank, so to speak. We are what we eat. Stay away from sugar, salt, alcohol. Everyone knows that cigarettes are hazardous to your health. Try to eat less fried foods. We all tend to overeat. It is easy to put weight on the stomach line and hard to get it off. Enough said!

This next series of exercises is called a tri set, because it is a combination of three different exercises that work on the same muscle group. The stomach should be worked from various angles. Try for 10 to 20 reps of each exercise in the tri set.

The starting position is flat on your back, heels and hands as close together as possible, toes pointed.

Sit up and bring your feet as close to your body as possible. Keep your back straight. Clasp your wrists and with your forearms keep a tight grip on your legs. Inhale as you sit up. Try to keep your feet together.

Another variation is the leg raise. As you sit up, reach forward and try to touch your ankle. Alternate the legs on each repetition. Remember to point the toes.

This is a front view of the same technique. Bring your leg up as high as possible. Balance and timing are the major components of this exercise.

Another variation is the side leg raise. Inhale on the start of the upward motion. Exhale on the downward action. Use your hands to maintain balance and support for this exercise. Start with your legs together.

Use your arm and hand for support, just as you would to watch television on a bed. The right hand provides support for the head; the left hand stabilizes the body.

This tri set is called the crab. This drill can be broken down to the individual exercises. The tri set is very difficult to do. Each exercise helps build a strong and flexible midsection.

The last warm-up exercise is the push-up. The push-up works the upper-body muscles. The chest, back, and arms are the basic groups of muscles used in this exercise. There are two different hand positions for the push-up. I recommend the hands close together with the thumb and forefinger touching. Some people do the push-up with the hands spread to about shoulder width, but it is my opinion that this works more of the chest muscles, instead of concentrating on the punching muscles of the arm and shoulder.

Starting position: Lie flat on the floor, resting on your fore-arms and hands. Inhale before you start to push your weight up.

Extension phase: Exhale as you push up. Inhale before exerting force. Close hand position increases the arm workout.

3
MARTIAL ARTS PSYCHOLOGY

Psychology is the science of the human mind in any of its aspects, operations and powers, or functions. Martial arts psychology must be used to help make you formulate an organized framework of reality. Your goals and priorities must be classified into three forms: mental, physical, and spiritual. Energy is classified in two types: positive and negative. As martial artists, we must use our logic and imagination to the best of our ability. A positive mental attitude combined with high spiritual expression is the best formula for human development. Martial arts develops all of my potential. My proficiency in the arts is strictly a byproduct. My clear thinking and spiritual contentment are clearly the most functional part of my development in the arts.

Below is a table that will help to simplify some of my theories of behavioral conditioning. Develop good habits and drop all bad habits. Our goal as human beings is to make the best of the time given to us on this planet. Go to school! Stay in school! Learn all that you can. Life is a series of experiences, good and bad. We learn from both.

OBJECTIVES GUIDELINE

MENTAL	SPIRITUAL	PHYSICAL
Clear thinking	Constant energy flow	Biocomputer, suspension system, and compressor development
Objective and subjective thinking	Positive energy	
	Remain calm during crises	
Good habits	Breathing techniques (kata)	Good eating habits and exercise
Feeling good about yourself		
Formulating a good framework of reality		Aerobic and cardiovascular exercise programs (jogging, swimming, martial arts, jumping rope)
Plan your work, work your plan		

Bruce Lee, *The King of Kung Fu*

Martial arts can be a lifelong learning experience. I know it has been that for me. I will never stop learning. We must know what we want from the martial arts to determine how to achieve our goals. Most people come into the martial arts because of negative forces in our environment. Violence has become epidemic. Therefore, people try to protect themselves with guns, knives, Mace, and tear gas. None of these really work; the mind is the most effective weapon. If your mind is tuned up, you can sense danger, and therefore avoid it. In the Ron Van Clief System, we have a mechanism called psychophysical drills. These drills are used to develop and stimulate the mind and the body at the same time. Psychophysical drills help to organize the basic principles of human engineering and systematic logic. The development of one's potential is the most important part of the training process.

There are five theories of martial arts psychology. These theories make up the basic understanding of the self.

Martial arts psychology starts with the personality theory. This is the most intricate part of the human expression mechanism. Our personalities are the windows through which the public can observe our feelings. Most people feel defenseless at that point. Our actions express our desire to be important, or at least feel important. Personality is the expression of how we feel about ourselves. Genetics, diet, and environment control our personalities. Some people are easygoing, while others are volatile. Stress and pressure created by the rituals of civilization constantly bombard our senses with a myriad of stimuli. We react to environmental changes. (If you feel cold, you put on a sweater.) Role playing has become a universal pastime. Shakespeare said we are all actors on the world stage. Keep your good habits, break your bad habits. Martial arts is life. Self-expression is how we live, feel, and think.

There are only two types of personalities: positive and negative. Positive people are constructive. Negative people are destructive. Personality is either positive or negative energy. We live and change from day to day. When there is no change, there is no progress.

The second of the basics of martial arts psychology is the learning theory. Learning is a combination of innate ability and behavioral conditioning. We learn from experience. We must practice all skills to achieve and maintain proficiency. Everyone is a product of previous societies. The human animal has progressed from caveman time to satellites on the moon. What is man searching for? It is an integral part of man's personality to explore this environment. When man has pioneered the last uninhabited planet, what will be next? Learning skills are inputs to the biocomputer (the human brain). Inputs become applied skills. You must first like the desired subject in order to stimulate the right attitude for optimum learning potential.

We learn by experiencing our environment from infancy to form our own perspectives. Change is constant because of the many varied stimuli affecting our environment. Learning is caring about yourself. We learn good habits and bad habits. Negativity changes the state of the mind. Learning cannot always be an enjoyable experience. Negative as well as positive experiences have shaped my life. The good and the bad have enabled me to see myself realistically. Learning anything is under-standing the basic concept. We all learn by on-the-job training! It is important to have a guideline to understand our own abilities. Learning is "Plan your work, work your plan."

Psychoanalytic theory is the third part of the programming mechanism. The ability to analyze the mind comes only when one understands motivation. Motivation is caused by stimulus that is either biochemical or external in nature. We all have the same goals and dreams: peace, security, and comfort. Everyone has his own way of attacking problems. Solutions overcome problems. A solution might be something as simple as organizing and setting one's priorities. The problem of economics is the cause of most stress. We need money to exist. To provide for yourself and your loved ones takes a great deal of money. Our lives are thousands of days of work. Most people work until they die. This is reality. If you are in school, stay there. You will need all the knowledge you can get. Know yourself and know your environment.

Explore your own potential. Go for it! You never know until you try. Motivation is understanding yourself. If you know why you do things, you understand yourself. Organize your framework of reality. Know what you want, then find out how to get it.

Our fourth theory is the cultural theory. Our cultural backgrounds have a great deal to contribute to our overall attitudes. Most ethnic groups stick together, which is natural. Every culture has positive and negative aspects. Only the strong survive! Who are you? Where are you? Where did you come from? These are the important questions. It is important that we know the answers. We must understand our cultural heritage. I believe we are of one race—the human race.

Last, there is the behaviorist theory. All people strive to exist in a comfortable manner. Life is short! We are all conditioned animals. We live by the experiences and accumulated knowledge of our ancestors. Natural man in an abnormal society. Man has been at war with nature to survive since the beginning of time. We all adapt to the environment to survive. The human mind is millions of brain cells that elevate man from just being another animal on the planet. Humans, the thinking animals. We are the same as any other animal. We do what we have to in order to survive. Future societies will consider today's modern man quite primitive. Everything is relative. Survival is the main instinct we have in common with the animals of prey. The human mind uses logic and imagination to adapt to the environment.

These five theories constitute the basis of martial arts psychology. All of these theories help develop the potential of the human being. Self-expression corrects the imbalance between good and bad stimuli.

THEORIES OF MARTIAL ARTS PSYCHOLOGY

1. Personality theory: Self-expression.
2. Learning theory: There is no end to learning.
3. Psychoanalytic theory: Mind power (logic plus energy and deductive analysis).
4. Cultural theory: Know yourself and your environment.
5. Behaviorist theory: Systematic logic and creative imagination.

CHINESE GOJU LOGIC—
PSYCHOPHYSICAL PRINCIPLES
AND THEORY

Defeat the self, first, to know: getting ready for combat takes mental and physical preparation. The mind and the body have separate realities. Our minds tell our bodies what to do. Our bodies respond with the correct physical action. If we are structurally able to react, it will be with the body's potential. Our limits are our body's limitations. Fat is not muscle. Our mental attitude (the iron will) trains our bodies. As you progress, your body dictates your tactics and strategy. Keep your mind and body in proper synchronization. Know your limitations; this is the difference between reality and fantasy. Once you come to terms with your biomechanical abilities, your mind designs different assault strategies, as your body executes the tactics. Strategy + Tactics = Applied Chinese Goju Logic (S + T = CGL). Set a goal. Be realistic. Plan your work. Work your plan. The biomechanical process is the integration of the mental and physical components of our total being. Our brains are living computers charged by our mental outputs and inputs. The brain controls not only the sensory processes but the total physicality of our psyche. The brain is like a dynamo. The brain's energy supplies the limbs with the correct messages to enact reflexive psychophysical mechanisms. If the sync between our computers and our limbs is not correct, we will not use the proper martial arts technique. First, the heart and lungs need strengthening for stamina and endurance. Our muscles, tendons, and ligaments need daily maintenance. Without this necessary daily maintenance, it is impossible for total mental and physical output. Our bodies know only the past and the present. During our life cycle, we depend on our bodies to carry us through this life into the next. Your body is the temple in which your soul and spirit live. When the mind is in good running order, the body will follow. Mental Input + Physical Output = Optimum Results.

4
CLOSE-RANGE WEAPONS

Close-range weapons refer to hand techniques. Legs are longer than hands. It is best to categorize techniques in order of their striking range. Hand techniques work in almost every situation. Leg techniques are somewhat limited. No one can execute flying kicks in a telephone booth. Realistically speaking, hand techniques work much better than leg techniques. Your hands are naturally faster than your legs. Leg techniques take a lot of maintenance. That means hard work. I prefer hands to legs in self-defense situations. Of course, it is best to use what you feel most comfortable with. Some people like legs, others like hands. There are five basic hand strikes in the Ron Van Clief System taught to White Belts.

One of the most devastating punchers that I can bring to mind is sensei Earl Monroe. Earl is a very aggressive fighter. He is a former United States champion in sparring. In the early 1960s Earl broke two of my ribs in a sparring match. This accident happened while we were in the dojo (temple of martial arts teaching) practicing for a tournament. Earl has always been known for his ferocity and tenacity. I appreciate all the Zen lessons that I received from Earl. He will always be my good friend and martial arts brother.

The first of the hand techniques is the sunfist punch. This punch is used in most of the kung fu and karate systems in practice today. It is one of the fastest punches in my system. In the finished position the palm is facing down and the fingers are on the inside. The hand is relaxed until the point of contact.

Bruce Lee loved the speed of the sunfist. He thought it was the quickest punch in his style. Bruce introduced me to the style of wing chun boxing, which combines the snake and the crane styles of kung fu. Bruce combined many different forms of combat to finally create his own form, Jee Kune Do: the way of the intercepting fist. Bruce's style was not a classic form, but it was effective. The bottom line is the effectiveness of the techniques!

SUNFIST PUNCH

Form

This is the preparatory position for all the basic hand techniques. Both arms are close to the rib cage for protection. Your hands are closed but not tightly. Relax your body.

Extend your right sunfist to a position directly in front of you. This is called the centerline position. Make sure that you keep your hand closed as you extend your arm. Do not punch with a loose hand. That would without a doubt cause self-injury.

This side view allows a better line of sight for technique. Notice how the left hand guards the body. Keep your back straight! Always keep your eyes on your target. Never drop your guard. Keep your weight evenly distributed.

In this side view the left punch is demonstrated. Make sure that the right hand is in the guard position.

Recommended Reps: 20 to 100 on each hand alternately. If weights or light dumbbells are used, high repetitions are suggested. Always practice at least 20 repetitions.

Practical Applications

A left sunfist combined with the right grab-and-pull mechanism. Note: The left shoulder shifts in the direction of the striking force. Punch and pull! The sunfist can be used at close and medium range. Suggested targets: face, neck, throat, groin, and breathing system.

The left sunfist to the breathing system, while pulling with the right grab. Pull into the punch! Always move your body in the direction of the striking force.

Training Aids

Small targets develop accuracy, timing, and focus. Moving targets are best.

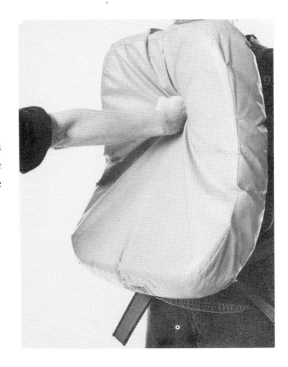

This Everlast shield allows for full-extension techniques with a moving target. Techniques should be practiced with a positive mental attitude. Training aids help to develop good technique and quick reflexes.

CORKSCREW PUNCH

Form

Starting position: Both hands should be closed and in a tight chamber, which is the position in which the forearm is parallel to the floor and the sides of the fist are on the side of the body. Keep your legs spread at shoulder width. Bend your legs for support.

Extend your right corkscrew punch in a straight line directly to the center of your body. This position is called the centerline form. As your right hand extends forward into a tight fist, keep the left hand in a tight chamber. Keep your back straight. Exhale as you punch.

Extend your left corkscrew punch straight to the centerline. Your right hand goes directly to chamber as you punch with the left. Both arms work in a pulley action to amplify the hit power of your technique. Make sure the transitions are smooth and fast. Practice punching with both hands to develop a natural flow of technique.

The side view shows how the left hand goes directly to chamber as the right hand punches. Always keep your back straight and shoulders aligned. The shoulder-width stance is the most useful stance for practicing the hand techniques of the Van Clief System.

Practical Applications

The corkscrew punch is a strong hand technique. It is very common in the various karate and kung fu systems existing today. Try to keep your forearm close to the side of your body until the last moment. Your forearm and elbow guide the punch to the target with a smooth and flowing action.

The Corkscrew Punch in Action

The left corkscrew punch connects to the chin. This technique affects the neck and spinal cord. Use your body and shift in the direction of the force line. Always move in the direction of the punch. Your legs provide the stationary foundation necessary for full-power punches. Never drop your guard. Pick your targets by priority. The easiest target for the corkscrew punch is the chin. It is an excellent setup technique; simply combine the corkscrew punch with alternate hand and leg techniques. When the corkscrew is executed with the front hand, it is similar to the boxer's jab. I use the jab to set off other combinations.

Training Aids

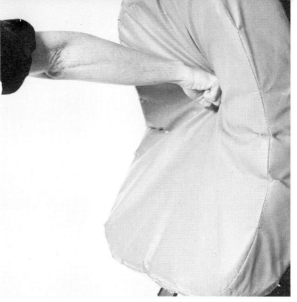

The Everlast shield is an excellent aid to training. It permits full contact without physical injury. Everlast produces a complete supply of training equipment used in boxing and football that is very useful in the martial arts. Heavy bags, speed bags, and jump ropes are necessary to become effective in the martial arts. Remember that techniques practiced in thin air are just that! Techniques must be practiced against resistance. Dumbbell and hand weights help immensely with hand speed and power. It is my firm opinion that progressive resistance is a necessary part of any martial arts training regime.

Training and Applications

Try practicing the left corkscrew punch with Heavy Hands. Heavy Hands are an excellent addition to our training schedule. AMF Heavy Hands allow full use of the fingers while exercising. Heavy Hands also have variable resistance.

The right corkscrew punch is practiced in a fluid motion. Your arms are like pulleys. Always remember to keep one hand in the defensive position. The shoulder-width stance is the Ron Van Clief System standard for the practice of all hand techniques in the White Belt workout.

Recommended reps: From 3 to 5 pounds is suggested. 25 to 50 performed with both hands.

REVERSE CHOP

Form

Starting position: The shoulder-width stance with open hands is the ready posture. Keep elbows close to the rib cage.

Prepare by elevating the left forearm to a level above the chest. Your right hand is in the guard position as usual. Keep fingers straight so as not to incur injury. This is the initiation phase of this action.

This is the extension phase of the action. Your left hand moves in a parallel action to a right angle from your chest line. Relax your shoulder and arm muscles. Your right hand is in the guard position as the left hand executes the reverse chop. Always look in the direction of the force line. Turn the body slightly in the direction of the strike.

Preparatory position for the other side. Remember, all techniques are practiced on the right and left sides. The right forearm moves to a position parallel to the floor. The left hand assumes the guard position. Keep the elbow of the guard arm close to the rib cage for protection.

This is the output phase of the action. Always turn in the direction of the force line. Stepping or shifting the body at the same time allows full commitment in technical execution. As the right hand chops, the left is in the standard guard position.

Training Aid

The Everlast shield is again used to demonstrate the various hand techniques. Make sure that you tuck in your thumb and straighten your fingers.

Recommended reps: At least 20 techniques with each hand. Suggested targets: Neck, throat, groin, breathing system, and leg joints.

The Reverse Chop in Action

The reverse chop to the throat. The left hand pulls as the right hand strikes.

SPEARHAND/SNAKE FIST

Form

The snake is one of my favorite animal forms. Speed, flexibility, and accuracy are the qualities gained from practicing snake techniques. Snake mechanisms attack only the weak and vital targets: eyes, neck, throat, groin, and skeletal system. The joints are the major targets in snake attacks. Constriction and control are the basic mechanisms used in the different snake techniques. Chokes, locks, and levers are my favorite snake techniques. Grandmaster Peter Urban is one of the finest practitioners of aiki jitsu. Snake techniques are standard devices in aiki jitsu. Aiki jitsu is one of the ninja arts taught to me by Grandmaster Urban. In the past three decades, I have seen hundreds of different snake techniques. Most are too complicated to understand! A snake bites, holds, and chokes its victims. This is the basis of the snake techniques in the Ron Van Clief System.

The shoulder-width stance is the normal stance for hand techniques. The right hand attacks as the left hand guards. Attacks with alternate hands are optimum. Speed and accuracy! This side view provides a different perspective from the frontal. Relax and breathe normally.

Your legs are slightly bent for stability. Shoulders are straight in line with the body. The left elbow protects the rib cage while the forearm and hand guard the head area.

Recommended reps: 20 to 100

The Snake in Action

40

BACKFIST STRIKE

Form

The shoulder-width stance with the closed fist is the opening position. Spread your legs, but not wider than your shoulders! Keep your head up, back erect, and shoulders lined up. Relax and breathe normally. Prepare your mind for full control.

Mechanically, the backfist strike is almost identical to the reverse chop, except that the hand is open for the chop and closed for the punch. As the right hand attacks, the left guards. Bend the legs for a stable stance. Always close your fist tightly as you extend your striking hand.

Your left hand attacks as the right hand moves to the guard. Always look in the direction of the strike. Your opponent could move and you would have to change your technique. Always be aware and never lose eye contact.

The Backfist Strike in Action

The right backfist strike to the temple is ideal. Keep your defending hand in the guard position. Remember to always be on offense *and* defense! Always move or shift in the direction of your strike force line.

The right backfist strike with the left guard posture. I am moving downward toward my target. Exhale as your hand moves toward the target. Inhale as you cock the arm for the strike.

Training Aid in Practice

The backfist strike practiced on the Everlast shield. Remember to tuck in your thumb and maintain a tight fist. Never lose eye contact with your target.

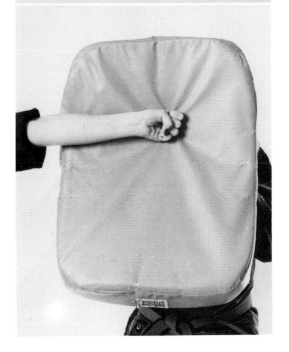

5
LONG-RANGE WEAPONS

Long-range weapons refers to leg techniques. Your legs are longer than your arms. Kicking techniques are very useful when closing the distance. I believe that kicking mechanisms are necessary to complete your personal arsenal.

In the past three decades I have seen some of the greatest kickers in the art of karate. At the top of the list is Bill Wallace. Bill is one of the flashiest kickers on the tournament scene. I have had the opportunity to spar with Bill on a few different occasions. His left leg possessed great speed and accuracy. Remember, kicking techniques require room to execute. Bill's left leg won him many honors. Bill and I fought the match of the century on July 16, 1977. Although this was billed as a full-contact match, it wasn't. This match lasted a couple of rounds. I was able to sweep Bill in the first round. His left leg was really quick that day. One of Bill's round kicks hit me on the right side of my temple. It was so fast that I didn't see it. The outcome of this match was a draw. It will always be one of my fondest memories. Bill is a great champion and friend.

The first of the long-range weapons discussed in this chapter is the round kick.

ROUND KICK

Form

Starting position: Relax and breathe normally. You are in the standard shoulder-width stance. Remember to move your hands to the guard position when you get in range. Raise your leg into a tight chamber. Beverly Stowe demonstrates the proper form of the round kick.

The extension phase of this kick is the most important. Not only does your body turn in the direction of the kick, your supporting leg shifts forward with the kick. You are striking with the instep or the shinbone of the kicking leg. Always look in the direction of your attack!

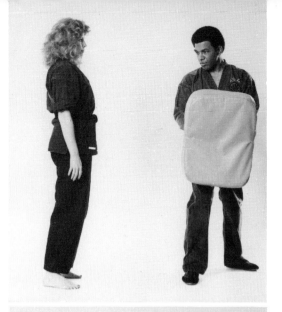

Starting position is the shoulder-width stance. Look at your target. Make sure that you are close enough to reach your target. The most common mistake when using kicking mechanisms is not being close enough. This exposes you to attack. It takes time to move your leg out and back to the original position.

Chamber the right leg. Keep your hands in the guard position. Inhale and prepare to put all your power and speed into the kick.

This is the extension phase of the kick. Turn your body in a semicircular action toward the kick. Make sure to pivot the left leg in the direction of the right kick. Do not bend the toes of the kicking leg!

This close-up shows how the foot should kick the target. Your foot should be flush on the target. Make sure to turn and kick with speed and accuracy. It takes a lot of discipline to kick with power and speed. This Everlast shield is used to practice kicking the body. Smaller targets are used for face kicking. Always use a constant forward motion when delivering kicking mechanisms.

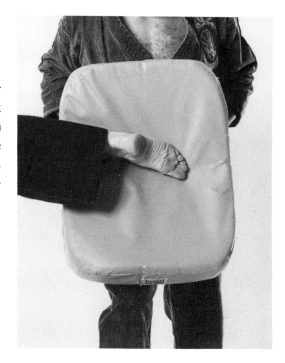

This detail shows the proper form for round kicking. Small targets take greater focus and accuracy to hit. Always use a moving target to develop accuracy and timing. I find the round kick is one of the easiest kicks in the Van Clief System. It is a fluid semicircular action that makes it easy to deliver. The round kick is a right-angle kick with the instep or the shinbone as the striking surface. In some styles, practitioners use the ball of the foot. In the street it is almost impossible to pull back your toes in shoes. Exhale in the extension phase.

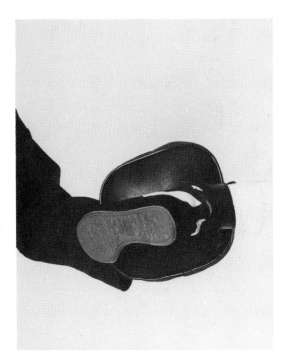

The Round Kick in Action

The body round kick is an excellent counter for a face punch. It is easier to hit the body than the head with a kick. You lose power the higher you kick. Low kicks work best. Of course, it is best to practice kicking all three areas—low, medium, and high. Kicks work best when you create an opening.

This is the jumping round kick. It is very effective in action. Jump kicks are surprise attacks. The kick and the jump are accomplished at the same time. Keep your hands in the defensive guard position.

FRONT KICK

Form

Starting position: Inhale as you bring your right leg to chamber. Always keep your hands in the guard position. Beverly looks straight to the front. Bend your left leg to ensure stability. Remember, your supporting leg acts as a cushion to absorb the shock of the impact force.

This is the full output phase of the kick. Extend your leg straight to the front. Pull back your toes as you extend your leg. The target is the stomach or the groin area. This kick can be delivered in a split second.

This close-up shows the proper way for the foot to contact the body. Your heel is pulled back with the toes. Never kick with full speed without a point of contact. Practicing kicks in thin air develops speed only. You need a target to develop power and accuracy. It is best to do at least 10 to 20 reps with each leg.

48

BACK KICK

Form

Start with the leg in the chamber position. This kick is directly to your rear. The striking surface is the heel or the bottom of the foot. The target is the breathing system. When you bring your left leg to chamber, make sure the heel is pulled back under the knee. This action protects you as you are kicking.

Always look over the shoulder of the leg you are kicking with. Never kick without looking at your target. This could cause permanent knee and muscle damage. Never drop your hands from the guard position.

The Back Kick in Action

Here we see Chris attack Marcus with a rear grab. Relax and concentrate on speed, power, and focus.

Notice how Marcus turns his body in the direction of the kick. As the right leg extends, Marcus looks over his right shoulder at Chris. Keep the supporting leg bent for stability. Use speed and power to extend the leg toward the target.

REVERSE CRESCENT KICK

Form

The reverse crescent kick is one of the fastest kicks in this system. This kick travels in a semicircular path to the target. In your shoulder-width stance, extend your left hand. Remember to extend the fingers and tuck in the thumb. The striking surface of the foot is the outer edge of the sole. Sometimes the heel is used. With shoes on, both are effective. You are kicking the left palm with the left foot.

After the outer edge of the foot hits the left palm, continue the circular action back to the original position. This kick travels from the inside to the outside.

As the left leg starts to rise, the supporting leg is bent. To observe proper form, maintain the right hand chamber position. Remember, this is just the form for practice. Always keep your guard up! In the Chinese styles, this kick is sometimes called the half-moon kick.

The Reverse Crescent in Action

Relax! Remember to never lose eye contact. Be aware and loose as a goose.

Grab the wrist and control the extended arm. Your left hand pulls down on the elbow joint for control. This is called a trapping motion.

Pull downward and start the kicking action. Keep the supporting leg bent for balance and stability. Concentrate!

The outer edge of your foot contacts the lower abdomen or groin area. Maintain a tight grip for control. The reverse crescent kick must have a whiplike action.

Without putting the leg down, deliver a second kick to the face. Your right hand is in the guard position. Bend your right leg. Turn in the direction of the kick by pivoting your right foot.

CRESCENT KICK

Form

Extend your left hand to the centerline position. Your right hand is in chamber. Bend the suspension system for support. The crescent kick moves in the opposite direction of the reverse crescent. This is sometimes called the full-moon kick. The contact surface is the inside of the foot. The heel is also an excellent contact surface.

This kick travels in a semicircular path toward the target. Your left arm is extended to the centerline position. Keep your back straight.

Use your hip and leg muscles to amplify the hit power. Pivot your supporting leg in the direction of the kick. Try to touch your left hand with the heel of your right foot.

Snap the leg in a semicircular fluid motion upward to the target. After completion of the kicking action, lower the leg to the original position. Speed is the essence of the crescent kick.

Training Aid Practice Drill

The Young Dragon executes the left crescent kick on the kick pad. Never drop your hands from the guard position. Ron junior demonstrates the correct form for practice with the focus pad.

The Crescent Kick in Action

The crescent kick to the head is a very good technique. Always look in the direction of your techniques.

The crescent kick to the groin area is a hard kick to block. Remember, the crescent kick is like a whip.

SIDE KICK

The side kick is one of my favorites. Toyotaro Miyazaki and Luis Delgado were two of the fighters of the 1960s and 1970s who used the side kick with effectiveness. The side kick is best used for the middle and low targets. Only an expert can use the side kick to the face effectively. The striking surface is the heel or the outer edge of the foot. I tend to favor the heel myself. The heel is much stronger than the blade of the foot. The side kick is a great finishing technique for a barrage of upper-level attacks.

Starting position: From the shoulder-width position, the left leg goes directly to chamber. Your toes are pulled up. Both arms are in the defensive position. It is best to use an Everlast shield or bag to practice kicking mechanisms.

Extend your left leg toward the target. Always remember to look at your target. Bend your supporting leg to absorb the shock of the kick. The supporting leg acts as a shock absorber for all kicking techniques. Never take your eyes off your attacker.

Reverse angle: Kick with feeling! Emotional content! The heel of the supporting leg is pivoted in the direction of the kick.

Recommended reps: 10 to 15 reps with each leg.
Suggested targets: Knee, thigh, groin, middle level, and face.

Training Aid in Practice

This close-up shows the proper form of the side kick. The foot is parallel to the ground. Remember to pull the toes back to avoid injury.

Small targets increase accuracy and focus. The Pony grappler protects the foot and allows better stability for kicking. The heel of regular sneakers is too high for good support in kicking. Flat shoes or gymnastic slippers work better.

The side kick can be used against low-, medium-, and high-level targets.

6
IRON ELBOW KATA

1. Opening posture: The shoulder-width stance is the opening posture for all of the Chinese Goju forms. Your heels are together and hands are placed at the sides. Relax and concentrate on techniques.

2. Starting posture: The right hand is closed in a fist behind the left hand. Always relax and breathe before starting any kata.

60

3. Your left leg moves into the front stance as your left hand extends forward. Notice that your right hand is in a tight chamber. Seventy percent of your weight is placed on the left leg with 30 percent on the right leg. The technique with the left hand is called the spearhand to the throat. The spearhand is sometimes used as a grab. Keep your shoulders straight.

4. Your left hand pulls your opponent into the right elbow strike. The left hand is open and the right hand is closed into a fist. Keep the front leg bent and the rear leg straight. Relax and concentrate.

5. Slide the left hand directly across the right forearm to the fist. Don't lose contact with the right arm.

6. Pull your elbows down close to the rib cage. The right hand remains closed. Your left hand remains open with fingers extended.

7. Your left hand executes an iron palm strike to the head area. The right hand goes directly to chamber position. Keep your stance steady.

8. The left iron palm turns into a grab. Keep the shoulders aligned. Your right hand executes a monkey elbow to the rear.

9. Your left hand pulls your opponent into the right upward elbow strike. Both hands move at the same time. Make sure that your right elbow is moving in an upward direction.

10. Complete the right elbow strike. Your left hand goes directly into the chamber posture. Make sure that the elbow is pointed directly up.

11. Your right hand reaches toward the sky in preparation for the downward elbow strike. Always look straight ahead. Keep your body erect.

12. Your right elbow comes directly down to the centerline position. This elbow strike is used for the head or the back of the neck. Always exhale as you strike. Always have a positive attitude when executing techniques.

13. Prepare for the sideward elbow strike by pulling your right hand over to your left shoulder. Make sure that your right hand is closed in a clenched fist. Keep your left hand in the chamber position.

14. Your right arm moves quickly to the right, executing the sideward elbow strike. This strike is used against the side of your opponent's face or body. Make sure that the arm is parallel to the ground. Never take your eyes off your target. Remember that all the moves in kata are actual techniques.

15. Drop your right elbow to protect your rib cage. This action also prepares for the next technique.

16. Your right hand executes an uppercut strike to the face area. The best target is the chin. Always look at your target. Never take your eyes off your opponent.

17. Your right hand and right leg move forward. The right spearhand strike is combined with the right forward-stepping action. You are now in the right front stance. The left hand is in the chamber position.

18. You execute a left elbow strike as the right hand pulls in the direction of the strike. Remember to pull in the direction of your strike! You are now in the right front stance. Remember to keep your shoulders erect.

19. Slide your right hand across your left forearm. Keep both arms parallel to the ground.

20. Quickly move both elbows into the rib cage area for protection. This action also prepares for the next movement.

21. Your right hand executes an iron palm strike to the face area. Remember to keep your fingers straight and your thumb bent for protection.

22. The iron palm strike turns directly into a grabbing mechanism. Keep the left hand in the chamber. Make sure to keep a stable stance.

23. Your right hand pulls as the left elbow starts upward.

24. Complete your left upward elbow strike to the face. Keep your right hand in the chamber position.

25. Your left hand reaches for the sky. Prepare for the next strike, which is a downward elbow strike.

26. Execute the left downward elbow strike.

27. Pull your left hand over to the right shoulder. Make sure that your left hand is closed. Keep the right hand in the chamber.

28. Your next technique is the left sideward elbow strike. The target is the side of the head or the body.

29. Now your left elbow drops into the rib cage area for protection. This is also a preparatory action for the next technique, which is the left uppercut punch.

30. Your left hand executes an uppercut punch to your attacker's chin.

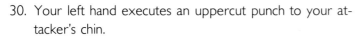

31. Your left hand moves directly into the spearhand to the throat. At the same time, your left leg forward into the front stance. The next ten movements are the same as steps 3 through 16.

32. Your left hand grabs in preparation for the right upward elbow strike. Always maintain a stable stance.

33. Your right elbow moves in line with the left grab-and-pull mechanism. Slide the left hand directly across the right forearm to the fist. Don't lose physical contact with the right arm.

34. Pull your elbows down close to the rib cage. The right hand remains closed. Your left hand remains open with fingers extended. Keep your back erect and shoulders aligned.

35. Your left hand executes an iron palm strike to the face. The right hand goes directly to the chamber. Keep your stance steady.

36. The left iron palm turns into a grab. Your right arm executes a monkey elbow to the rear.

37. Now your left hand pulls your attacker into the right upward elbow strike. Both hands move at the same time. Make sure that your right elbow is moving in an upward direction.

38. Complete the right elbow strike. Your left hand goes directly into the chamber position. Make sure that the elbow is pointed directly up!

39. Your right hand reaches toward the sky in preparation for the downward elbow strike. Always look straight ahead. Keep your body erect.

40. Bring your elbow directly down to the centerline position. This elbow strike is used for the head or the back of the neck. Always exhale as you strike. Maintain a positive mental attitude throughout your kata and technique workouts.

41. Prepare for the side elbow strike by pulling your right hand over to your left shoulder. Make sure that your right hand is closed in a tight fist. Keep your left hand in the chamber position.

42. Your right arm moves quickly to the right, executing the sideward elbow strike. This strike is used against the side of your attacker's face or body. Make sure that the arm is parallel to the ground. Never take your eyes off your target. Remember that all the movements in kata are actual techniques used in self-defense.

43. Drop your right elbow to protect your rib cage. This action also prepares for the next technique. Maintain a good front stance.

44. Now your right hand executes an uppercut strike to the face area. The best target is the chin. Hitting the chin will cause shock to the neck and spine. Always look in the direction of the strike. This is the last movement of this form. You next move to the original posture, as in step 1.

IRON ELBOW FORM APPLICATIONS

The spearhand strike used in picture 3 is demonstrated by sensei Radu Teodorescu in this application. Notice the parallel right hand chamber. This is the left front stance in action.

This is an example of the left uppercut punch to the chin. Step 30 shows the proper form for kata. In the practical application the opposite hand protects in any punching situation. Chris Wade shows how to use the uppercut punch to the chin. Always look in the direction of your strike.

Sensei Radu and the Young Dragon, Ron junior, demonstrate the left front stance. This is the movement in step 3. Smooth fluid footwork is necessary to make kata work. This movement is also a good stretch to warm up the hamstrings and the rear thigh biceps. Keep your hands on your hips when practicing this stretch.

The right front stance is exactly the same mechanically as the left side except for the opposite leg in use. Try to keep your back straight. Do at least 20 repetitions of this stretch with each leg.

The upward elbow strike is demonstrated in this application by Roscoe Born. Note the form of the pulling and striking mechanism. This is one of the classic techniques of the Ron Van Clief System.

Roscoe demonstrates the left downward elbow strike as the right pull-grab mechanism. The right front stance is used in step 26 of the kata form.

This is the application of the downward elbow strike on the Everlast shield. This shield allows full force and commitment in practicing technique. The shield is not hard enough to cause injury. Beverly Stowe demonstrates the application of the downward elbow strike on the shield. When practicing this technique, it is necessary to close the hand as the elbow descends. Let your body drop a little in the stance. Always use your weight to increase hit power.

Roscoe Born demonstrates the iron palm to the chin of Alfred Ng. The right hand controls the left hand. Step 7 shows the proper form. Pull your right hand to chamber as the left executes the iron palm strike. Maintain a good front stance while delivering the technique.

Beverly demonstrates the training drill form for the application of the front elbow strike. Her right elbow moves in a circular motion directly to the target. Use your whole body when practicing this mechanism. Make sure that the Everlast shield is held securely. You don't want to injure your assistant. Exhale when you deliver any technique.

7
NINJA AIKI FORM

1. Attention position: This is the ready position for all the forms in the Van Clief System. This is the posture that enables you to start your "clear thinking." The Japanese have a saying that covers this: *Mizu no kokoro*. "Mind is like water" is the closest translation.

2. Yoi position: This and the next picture demonstrate the yoi. It is a combination of a right back fist and a left spearhand to the throat. Maintain a good shoulder-width stance.

3. This is the end of the yoi. Use dynamic tension in the arms, shoulder, chest, and back. At the final stage of this posture, relax the body and concentrate on focus.

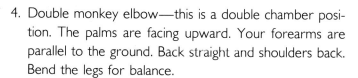

4. Double monkey elbow—this is a double chamber position. The palms are facing upward. Your forearms are parallel to the ground. Back straight and shoulders back. Bend the legs for balance.

5. Escape and evasion—the double aiki palms evade a double wrist grab. Push the hands straight down to the floor. Make sure that your fingers are not lower than your palms. Your hands should be approximately three or four inches away from your body.

6. Double palm-up blocks. This is also an escape from a double wrist grab. Move from the downward palms directly to the upward palm blocks. Keep your elbows as close to your body as possible.

7. Double high block. This mechanism has various practical applications. It can be used to escape a front lapel grab. Both arms move directly upward to a position over the head. Keep your fingers straight and your thumb tucked in to avoid injury.

8. This movement is exactly the same as step 6. The double palm-up block is a very fluid movement. You must be sure to keep fingers straight and thumbs tucked in. This is a good self-defense technique. It can be used with one or both hands at the same time.

9. The next movement is the twin mantis fist. You strike directly to your side. Slightly turn your body 90 degrees to the left. This double strike is with the back of the hands. Make sure to keep your arms close to your body.

10. The next mechanism is the double butterfly palms in the same direction as your mantis strikes. Always look in the direction of your techniques.

11. You next strike to the opposite side with the twin mantis fist. Remember to keep your arms close to your body.

12. The right double butterfly palms is the next mechanism in the ninja aiki form. All strikes and blocks are executed on both sides. Maintain a good shoulder-width stance.

13. The iron wall posture is the next position. Your right arm is perpendicular to the ground. Your left arm is parallel to the ground. The tip of your elbow is on the back of your left palm. This mechanism protects the upper and lower levels at the same time.

14. Closing the book is a trapping hands mechanism. Trapping hands neutralizes attacks. Your right and left forearms hold your attacker's arms. Make sure to maintain a tight grip on your attacker's forearms or wrists.

15. Both hands go directly to the double monkey elbow position. This is a good preparatory movement for an attack with both hands.

16. The twin dragon palms are the next technique. Your right palm strikes the face and your left strikes the lower area. Both strikes are accomplished at the same time.

17. The left iron wall is the next posture. Your left arm is perpendicular to the floor as your right forearm is parallel to the ground.

18. Closing the book is the next technique. Your left hand slaps your right forearm to maintain control. This is a trapping hands mechanism. This series is exactly the same as in steps 13 to 16. Remember, in the ninja aiki form all techniques are done with both hands.

19. The next technique is a retraction. Pulling your hands directly back into the chamber position allows them to be free. Another application would be the elbow strike directly to the rear.

20. Both hands then move into the twin dragon palms posture. The left hand strikes high and the right strikes low. Prepare to move directly to the closing posture.

21. The closing posture is the yoi position: the right backfist and the left upward spearhand. Remember to be in a good shoulder-width posture. Clear your mind.

22. End of form. Return to the original posture as in step 3.

Practical Applications

Double wrist grab countered with the double palm-up block. This is called an internal rotation. Both hands move out to rotate the elbows in. The palms rotate outward to create an acute angle on your attacker's wrists. Mike Angelone grabs my wrist. I turn my palms and my elbows inward to escape the grab.

Variation

The double wrist is countered with the double mantis fist. There are numerous escapes and evasions in ninja aiki. Remember to let your body work for you. Speed is the essence of aiki.

8
TENCHU
(Heaven's Breath Form)

1. Opening posture: This is the ready position for all kata. It is sometimes called the standing meditation. This position is the beginning and the end of all katas in the Ron Van Clief System. Relax and breathe.

2. This move is part of the dynamic tension in the opening of all Ron Van Clief katas. It is the first in a two-part opening called the yoi. *Yoi* is a Japanese word meaning a mental state of readiness. Inhale as you bring the right fist to meet the left palm. Speed is of the essence.

3. This is the point at which you start to exhale as you increase the muscular contraction of the various muscle groups. The chest, arms, stomach, and back muscles are tensed at the same time. The shoulder-width stance is used for the yoi posture.

4. Your left arm moves to the upward palm blocking mechanism. Your right hand is in the defensive guard posture. From the shoulder-width stance move to your left 90 degrees with your left leg. At the same time, pivot your right foot in the direction of the left leg. The block and the guard are executed at the same time. This is a short front stance.

5. Your left hand goes directly from the block to the grab mechanism. This is part of the snake style. The right hand moves directly to chamber. This chamber is also a monkey elbow striking to the rear. Maintain your left front stance.

6. Your left hooking block becomes a pull-grab mechanism. Move forward to a right front stance with a right iron palm. Remember to pull in the direction of your hit power.

7. Your right leg executes the preparatory cross-step motion. This action sets you up for a 180-degree turn. Keep the right arm extended until the turn is initiated.

8. The cross step has turned you to the right side. You are now in a right front stance. The right hand is in the upward palm block position. Your left hand protects the body and face. Remember, 70 percent of your weight is on the front leg, 30 percent on the rear leg.

9. The right hand turns into a hooking block as the left arm moves to the chamber. Bend your right leg and straighten your left. Pull your left hand sharply back to the chamber position. Your right hand is a hooking block.

10. Your left side moves forward with the left iron palm to the face, your right hand to the chamber position. This stance is called the left front stance. Keep your shoulders straight and back erect.

11. Your left leg shifts to the original position, 90 degrees to the left side. At this time your left hand blocks with a palm-up block. Keep your right hand in the centerline guard position.

12. The left palm-up block switches to a left hooking block. Keep your legs flexed for balance. The shoulder-width stance is a resting posture. Look straight to the front.

13. Explode with a right sunfist punch to the face area. Note that the left hand is closed and guarding the body. Your right foot and right hand work together. Keep your footwork smooth and fluid.

14. Now your left side moves forward with the left sunfist punch. Your right hand guards your body as you punch. There must be offense and defense at the same time.

15. The next punch is the last in the three-punch combination. Your right side moves forward with a sunfist. Naturally, the left hand and forearm provide the guarding mechanism.

16. You are now in a left front stance. The right hand guards the body as the left hand is the block. Relax and keep a smooth and natural pace.

17. The left hand attacks the eyes with the snakefist. The right guard is stationary. Maintain the left front stance. Keep the fingers of the left hand straight.

18. The right sunfist follows the left snakefist. Your left hand now becomes your guard. Keep your back erect.

19. Maintain your stance in this punching combination. Your left sunfist punch strikes the face, while your right hand is in the guard position.

20. Turning to right with both hands ready. You move your right leg to the right to pivot 180 degrees. You are now in a right front stance with the left hand in the guard position. Your right hand blocks with an open-hand slapping block. Maintain a good stance.

21. Your right snakefist strikes the eyes. Keep your left hand in a guard position. Your left hand is prepared for the next technique.

22. Your left sunfist attacks the face area. The right hand becomes the guard. Remember that all three of these techniques are in a stationary position.

23. The right sunfist attacks the chin. Your left hand becomes the guard. Keep a fluid and smooth pace to your combination. You must explode with your technique.

24. Reverse angle, the crane stance with both hands blocking. You are on your right leg. The right hand guards the upper area as the left hand blocks the middle area.

25. Your right crane stance hides many techniques. The right hand faces the right and the left hand faces the left. Your left knee is **in** attack. In the right crane stance all the extremities are working at the same time. Both legs and arms have separate jobs to do.

26. From the right crane stance you move into the left back stance. In the back stance you are ready for the next offense or defense. Your right forearm is parallel to the ground, and the palm faces the left in a chopping action.

27. This is the preparatory posture for kicking techniques. Both arms guard the body. Prepare yourself for a three-kick combination. You are in a left stance.

28. Execute a right front kick to the midsection. Both hands stay in the defensive guard position. Bend the left leg for stability.

29. Moving forward into a left front kick. Keep your guard up. Never lose sight of your target. Keep your back straight; avoid leaning backward when kicking.

30. The right front kick is the final kick in this three-kick combination. All three front kicks are done at full speed. Make the transition from the right and left as smoothly as possible.

31. Upon completing the right front kick, move into a right front stance with a right monkey elbow. The left hand is open and the right is closed. Maintain a good stance. Keep your back erect.

32. Side view. Note: Keep your shoulders straight. Keep the weight on the forward leg. Your left hand pushes your right elbow to the rear. This is the monkey elbow.

33. Pivot to the left 90 degrees, into a left front stance. Your left arm executes an overhead block, and the right hand punches with a corkscrew punch.

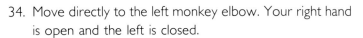

34. Move directly to the left monkey elbow. Your right hand is open and the left is closed.

116

35. Execute a right crossover step. This is the preparatory position just before you move to the right front stance. Prepare to turn 180 degrees to the right.

36. After the 180-degree turn to the right stance, execute a right overhead block with a left corkscrew punch to the middle area. Keep the weight forward in the front stance. Your knee should be over your toes. This is the last move in this form. Prepare to move back to the closing posture, which is the same as in step 2.

37. You are now completing tenchu form with the traditional yoi posture. The left hand is open and the right is closed in a fist.

38. End of form.

SELF-DEFENSE DRILLS

Zosia counters the choke of Glen. Relax and concentrate on your technique. Self-defense drills help to develop reflexes, timing, and attitude.

Zosia executes a thumb lock as she delivers a front kick to the pelvic area. Try to use hand and leg mechanisms together.

Finish off your attacker with a side kick in the stomach. Combinations are the secret of success in self-defense and sparring. Make your techniques sharp and strong.

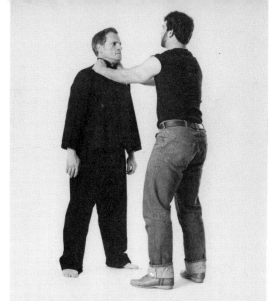

Maurice counters the choke of Brian. A front choke is a common street attack, so be prepared. Never take your eyes off your attacker.

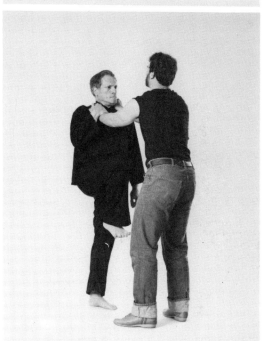

Maurice raises his right leg to the chamber position. This is the preparatory move for all kicking mechanisms in the Ron Van Clief System. At the same time, use your right hand to neutralize your attacker's left arm. Of course, these movements are done in a split second.

Maurice finishes Brian with a right kick to the knee combined with a left palm strike to the chin. Remember to use your hands and legs together. Exhale as you punch or kick.

Self-defense is important at any age. Relax—this is only a drill. Never lose eye contact with your attacker.

Grab with your left hand and execute a side kick to the knee. The side kick is with the bottom of the foot, as close to the heel as possible.

Ron junior demonstrates the side monkey elbow. Children have to pick targets closer to their height.

Lovely Libra Lederer demonstrates how to get out of a bear hug. It is almost impossible for a child to fight an adult. Therefore, surprise must be the weapon used to initiate the attack.

Both of your palms slap the ears in a quick motion. Try not to cup your hand. The palm should be as flat as possible. This technique will cause your attacker to drop you.

9
TRAINING TO WIN

Mr. Kong Fu Tak, founder of the Hong Kong Free Fighting Club in Kowloon, Hong Kong, is one of the best Thai boxers in Hong Kong today. Thai boxing is a form of martial arts that uses knees and elbows in competition. Elbows, knees, and low kicking attacks are the basic weapons of the kick boxer. I have found that Thai boxing is one of the most effective styles for competition. The training is rugged. At the Free Fighting Club, disco music accompanies all of the training sessions. The disco music creates a good steady pace for executing techniques. Timing and speed are very important in the training sessions. Each disco piece is about three minutes in length. There are always many different drills going on in the three-minute period. Sometimes, the heavy bag or speed bag is used to develop speed and pacing levels. Everyone works at the same time, no matter what exercises they are working on. This is a unique way to maintain pace and timing. I recommend the Hong Kong Free Fighting Club to anyone interested in real kick boxing. **Thai** boxers attack their opponent's legs in order to create instability in the fighting stance. Thai boxers can disable an attacker with just one well-placed kick to the thigh or knee. Thai boxers don't do kata or form, they only work training equipment like kicking pads and mitts. Each training session is a continuous series of footwork and offensive and defensive mechanisms. Special thanks to Kong and Victor Jauncey for their expert assistance with this segment on Thai boxing.

Competition falls into six categories: sparring, full contact/no contact, kata, empty-handed/weapons, breaking (boards, bricks, and cement slabs), and self-defense techniques. It is impossible to be proficient in all of these events. In the past three decades, I have competed in all six areas of competition. Most practitioners specialize in one of two areas: sparring and kata. Training for each event is totally different in methodology. Training methods change with each form of competition. My favorite form of competition is sparring. I really enjoyed some of the matches I had. Winning and losing are exactly the same thing. I look at competition as a form of practice. Sparring is the ability to use your techniques in a fluid and realistic manner. Full contact is much different from no contact. The people who do full contact don't look as sharp as the students of no-contact tournaments. In full contact, the knockout is the most important thing. Full contact is considered professional, whereas no contact or light contact is considered amateur. In amateur matches, the quality of the technique is the most important aspect. I really enjoyed competing in both full contact and no contact. Below is a list useful for sparring practice. The second chart is for kata.

SPARRING
Principles and Theories

1. Always keep your blocking system in working order.
2. Never take your eyes off your opponent.
3. Always train for competition; normal practice is not enough.
4. Heavy bag and speed bag training are a must.
5. Protective equipment is necessary during practice sessions.
6. Always have a positive mental attitude.
7. Never take your opponent for granted.
8. Speed, focus, and timing are necessary ingredients.
9. Always use both hands and legs in attacking and evasive movements.
10. Never stand still! Constant motion is the secret to success in sparring.

KATA
Principles and Theories

1. Always know every move well, before competing.
2. Always have a selection of different katas for competition. One kata is not enough.
3. Practice your katas every day, in order to develop a fluid execution.
4. Relate to kata as real techniques in motion.
5. If you make a mistake, keep going.
6. Never be intimidated by other well-known competitors.
7. Never perform in a dirty or sloppy uniform.
8. Remember that losing is part of competing.
9. Use that nervous energy to give a great performance.
10. Winners never quit, quitters never win.

THE AMERICANIZATION OF THE MARTIAL ARTS

Kong Fu Tak, founder of the Hong Kong Free Fighting Club

Ron Van Clief, 5-time world champion

Martial arts have changed from an Oriental discipline to an American sport. There have been many great practitioners of the martial arts who have changed the very essence of the arts. There are more karate tournaments in the United States than in all of the Orient. Two decades ago was the first real surge of tournament competition. Men like Ed Parker, Aaron Banks, Henry Cho, and Peter Urban have contributed greatly to the growth of the arts. There are at least three tournaments held every month in New York. The Amateur Athletic Union has become involved in national and international competitions. The martial arts have changed a great deal in concept and principle. The United States has been the forerunner in the martial arts competition. *The New York Times* has estimated that there are over ten million practitioners of the arts in the United States. New schools and styles are popping up all over. With the introduction of professionalism in the arts, politics has become a major part of competition. There should be an international organization that controls all tournaments and competitors. There are too many organizations, thus ruling out standardized rules for competition. The West Coast and the East Coast have completely different rules and regulations controlling competition. In the professional area there are two major forces behind contact karate. The Professional Karate Association (PKA) has worldwide coverage on satellite television. The PKA has been around for about seven years. I believe that the PKA is about the best at this time. The World Karate Association (WKA) is number two on the scene. Most of the WKA matches are held in Asia and Europe. The WKA is recognized in Asia as the top organization in sport karate. *Kick boxing* is the term that defines the contact area of the sport. *Contact karate* is incorrect because the fighters are restricted in the techniques and the areas of attack. In amateur competition, there is light contact and no contact. This is a good place to get the experience for the professional level.

It is too bad there really isn't any substantial prize money in the sport today. Soon, sponsors will realize the potential of the sport and start to explore its marketing capabilities. Martial arts are beautiful to observe. It is just a matter of time before the sport receives international recognition. Many kick boxers fight for minimal purses, sometimes under $50 per round. It really isn't worth it. It is too early to say that professionalism has ruined a noble art. Some of the best people in the arts no longer compete because of the politics and prejudices in the sport today. No one should take the chance of having his face kicked in for $50 per round. Imagine incurring a permanent injury for such a small purse! The purses will someday be comparable to boxing. Until then, the fighters will be ripped off by the promoters. In the 1960s, there was no prize money. Competition was great during that period. Many great American karatemen, such as Chuck Norris, Mike Stone, Joe Lewis, and Luis Delgado, devoted their lives to the arts for nothing. In those days, you paid your own way to tournaments. Today, if you are a rated competitor the promoters pay for your transportation. The trophies and medals were the only prizes until the early 1970s.

It is my opinion that the tournaments then were much more exciting to watch. Contact karate looks sloppy! Just going for the knockout changes the whole ideology of the sport. Contact karate has its place. I personally think that amateur competition will be around for a long time. It is going to be you, the practitioner, who decides the outcome of full contact versus no contact. Americans traditionally love to fight! The top fighters in full-contact and amateur competition are from the United States. I am very proud of this fact.

In the past three decades, I have observed the various changes in competition regulations. Some rules work; some don't. Eventually, there will be a national committee to regulate the various forms of the martial arts. With so many different factions, the competition scene is chaotic, to say the least. The PKA and the WKA have a big job ahead of them. Knowing the heads of these organizations personally, I know they can handle the job. Judy Quine is the head of the PKA, headquartered in Los Angeles. Howard Hanson is the head of the WKA, also in Los Angeles. I would like to commend both of these organizations for doing an admirable job, considering the obstacles. The Star System, endorsed by Chuck Norris, is one of the new organizations on the scene today. Good luck, Chuck!

Chuck Norris is the leading force on the martial arts movie scene. His movies have grossed millions of dollars internationally. It is really good for the sport to see real martial artists in the movies. Karate on the silver screen is a common sight today. Americans in the kung fu films have started a whole new era of action films. Kung fu movies have also infiltrated the satellite and cable television market. It has become a common sight to see kung fu movies on television. I never thought that they would make it to the tube! It is wonderful to see the martial arts flourish. In the past thirty years, I have had the opportunity to see the martial arts grow from obscurity to an international sport.

In this chapter, I would like to give credit to some of the great masters of American martial arts. My teacher Grandmaster Peter Urban has taught over twenty thousand students in the way of American Goju. Grandmaster Urban is the father of American karate. I have had the opportunity to study with him for over two decades. It is important to understand the history of American martial arts. I would need at least three chapters to really do justice to all the masters and experts who have brought the martial arts to where they are today. In the next volume, I will continue to list these twentieth-century samurai!

Another between-the-rounds shot at the World Championships in Hong Kong. I was the only American to make it from the eliminations to the finals on the second day. I weighed in at 163 pounds. It took me three weeks to come down from 182 pounds to make my division weight. In the finals I lost to a Yugoslavian opponent who weighed 179 pounds. Full contact is much different in the United States. There are no ropes as boundaries. The floor was wood-covered, with a loose canvas. Some opponents had four-ounce gloves; some had six-ounce gloves. Throws, chokes, and levers were allowed. It was a most exciting event. To train for this event, I jogged fifty miles a week for five weeks and worked out twice a day. Of course, my diet changed drastically—no junk food! My training consisted of heavy- and light-bag workouts. I would shadowbox six to eight rounds a day. Going from light heavyweight to middleweight was a great challenge in itself. Luckily, I didn't sustain any permanent injuries.

This shot was at the First International World Kung Fu and Freefighting Championship in Hong Kong. Each contestant fought in the eliminations and the finals the next day (May 1 and 2, 1982). Thirty countries were represented in this full-contact event. I placed second in the middleweight division. Although I didn't take first place, this event allowed me to express my mechanical and spiritual energies.

THE RON VAN CLIEF METHOD OF FULL-CONTACT TRAINING

1. Take control of the match immediately.
2. Explode with combinations . . . low and medium . . . high kill the body . . . open the head!
3. Uppercut/hook (low and high).
4. Straight punch with right cross/left hook.
5. Left hook/right cross (upstairs and downstairs).
6. Left hook to jaw/chin.
7. Double left hook . . . compressor and biocomputer.
8. Keep hands up! Offense and defense.
9. Duck punches to face and counterkick or punch to the body.
10. No fewer than ten punch combinations for knockout. Finish with sweep.
11. Let's go—keep going—there is nothing else—next!

10
RON VAN CLIEF FILMOGRAPHY

My film career started in the mid-1960s. I have always been a film buff. After being discharged from the Marine Corps in 1965, I joined the East Coast Stuntmen's Association (thanks go to Harry Madsen and Alex Stevens for their excellent training). My martial arts film career started in 1974 in the Philippines. I was discovered by Serafim Kafalexis of Madison World Films. This film, originally titled, *The Tough Guy*, was shot totally on location in the Philippines. It was to be the hardest job of my film career. The shoot took almost three months. I would get up everyday at 5:30 A.M. to prepare for the day's shooting. In Asia, there are no unions. You are either a cooperative actor or unemployed. We worked some days in excess of ten hours. Although it was mentally and physically exhausting, I was motivated to do my best. My part was a small one, but it allowed me to showcase my talents. At that time, I had been involved with the arts for more than fifteen years. The action director on the set asked me if I could do a side kick. This was my opportunity to show my stuff. The director, Mr. Tommy Loo Chun, was a former kung fu actor and stuntman. We developed a good working relationship of mutual respect. The cast was great, especially Jason Pai Piao, who became my good friend. Jason is now a big television star in Hong Kong. The first time I saw Jason was in the film *The Stranger from Canton*. It was produced in 1969 by Yangtze Films. It was Jason's debut. He really looked great. Jason and I would work out before and after the shooting schedule. *The Tough Guy* was soon to become *The Black Dragon*. Film producers change titles at will. Different markets and different titles! Remember, a film sells by the trailer, press book, promotional materials. The wrong title can kill a film. Serafim was taking a chance. *The Black Dragon* made more than six million dollars!

After *The Black Dragon*, I made five more films as the Black Dragon character. *The Death of Bruce Lee* and *The Way of the Black Dragon* were my two favorite Chinese films. In 1975, I shot a film, *The Super Weapon*, in New York City. This film will always be my favorite. *The Super Weapon* was the first real documentary on the subject of the martial arts. This film was a financial flop because the public goes to the movies to see the fantastic stuff. *The Super Weapon* dispelled all those silly myths about the martial arts. Working on *The Super Weapon* was my first time acting as a casting director and technical adviser. Some of the finest martial arts people I have ever met worked on *The Super Weapon*. All my films are available on video cassette.

In the past two decades, I have worked with some of the greatest names in the martial arts: Bruce Lee, Bruce Lei, Bruce Li, Carter Wong, Leo Fong, Masafumi Suzuki, Bill Louie, and a host of others.

In this chapter, you will see a collection of some of my favorite films. I hope you enjoy them! Martial arts films are fun. See them as sheer fantasy.

Black Dragon, a.k.a. *The Tough Guy,* Philippines, 1974. I lost sixteen pounds on
ation. Actors are just props.

Black Dragon, Manila. It was over 100 degrees in the shade—if you could find
me!

The Black Dragon

Dreams are reality!

The Black Dragon's Revenge, a.k.a. *The Death of Bruce Lee*, Hong Kong, 1975. La Pantera and the Black Dragon in action!

The Black Dragon's Revenge, New Territories, Hong Kong. I had met Charlie Bonet on Okinawa when I was a Marine. He is a great karateman and my good friend.

The Black Dragon's Revenge. We did this scene so many times I was almost in shock. My final scene with Thompson Kao Kong was the highlight of the film. I twisted his neck 360 degrees with an aiki jitsu technique. Cinematically it came off well.

The Black Dragon's Revenge. This was one of the beautiful days on location near a temple in the New Territories, Hong Kong. I created a form just for this scene. It was a synthesis of some of my favorite forms. It culminated with a twenty-five-tile break, which I insisted had to use real brick tiles. Most actors use phony tiles.

The Black Dragon's Revenge. In this shot I dispatch the villain, Dick Chan. Although Dick is no longer with us, he will always be remembered. Dick Chan was a veteran actor and stuntman. My counter for the face punch is the left grab and right tiger claw at the same time.

The Black Dragon's Revenge. In this scene, I was kicked in the jaw by Jason Pai Piao. It dazed me, but I finished the fight sequence. During the filming of *The Black Dragon,* Jason knocked out Thompson Kao Kong with a spinning reverse crescent kick.

The Black Dragon's Revenge. The villain is my good friend Angie Hok Lin. He was quite convincing in his role. He objected to having his hair shaved off. All in all, he was a pleasure to work with. A real professional!

RON VAN CLIEF AND DRAGON LEE, KUNG FU FEVER

Kung Fu Fever was filmed on location in Hong Kong and Korea. This production took fifty-eight days to complete shooting. The crew was Chinese, the talent Korean. I was the only foreigner on the film. Asian films are quite fascinating to act in. *The Death of Bruce Lee* and *Kung Fu Fever* were two of my favorite film projects.

Although the martial arts seen in films is unreal, it is entertaining. Kung fu films take a lot of time and energy. It is just like working out! There are really valid techniques used in the fighting sequences in film. Many film producers scout the local martial arts schools for talent. Sometimes, a student with potential is developed by the film companies. Many of my kung fu brothers in Hong Kong worked many years as stuntmen and extras just to get the opportunity to be seen by the film producers.

Kung Fu Fever

Kung Fu Fever, Korea, 1979. This film took fifty-eight days to shoot. We traveled from Seoul to Daugu. It was hot and dusty. Korea is a beautiful country. The port of Pusan was exciting. You can see some really good Tae Kwon Do in Korea. Korean film-making is much different from Chinese methods. All of the Korean stuntmen executed beautiful kicking techniques. Flying kicks and multiple kicking were standard procedure.

Dragon Lee and the Black Dragon in the final fight scene of *Kung Fu Fever*

Dragon Lee and I were just posing for some stills for the director. It was quite interesting playing a villain, after only playing good guys in the kung fu films. The part of a super-villain was an excellent opportunity to show my acting prowess.

This was one of the funnier stunts—trying to make the trampoline jump synchronize with an aiki jitsu throw. After a few technical difficulties, we made the shot in two takes. This was one of those ten-hour-day shoots, which is not uncommon in Asia. This was a very enlightening experience!

Carter Wong. Carter and I worked on the film *Way of the Black Dragon*. Carter is an expert in kung fu and Tae Kwon Do. He has appeared in more than sixty martial arts films. He was also a good friend of Bruce Lee. Carter is an outstanding actor and film director. We worked very well together.

Ron Marchini and Leo Fong. Leo Fong produced a film entitled *The Bamboo Trap*. This film was shot entirely in the Philippines. Leo was very helpful and supportive on this project. It was Leo Fong who first motivated me to write about the martial arts. Ron Marchini is a former United States champion and Hall of Fame member. Leo and Ron are pioneers who have developed the American martial arts scene. Below is an action shot from the picture.

KUNG FU FEVER—DRAGON LEE AND THE BLACK DRAGON IN ACTION

Bruce Lee—a good friend and great martial artist. He was the first real martial artist to get into the movies. He received international recognition in the late 1960s. *Enter the Dragon* was his contribution to the world of the martial arts. This film made Bruce Lee an international superstar. There will never be another like him.

Dragon Lee of *Kung Fu Fever*. Lee is an exponent of the Tae Kwon Do system of martial arts. His special training is in hapkido and the animal forms. Lee is a veteran of more than thirty films. We worked together for two months and I learned a great deal about the film business from him. We learned something about the martial arts from each other. He is a gentleman, and he has a good sense of humor.

APPENDIX
SUPERHEROES OF THE
MARTIAL ARTS

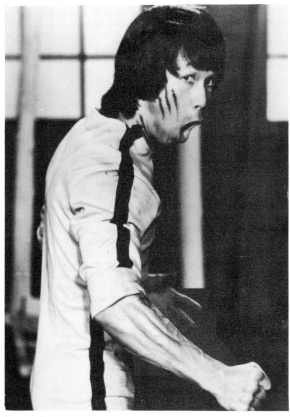

David Claudio, a former world karate champion (full contact). One of the new breed of martial artist experts, soon to be internationally recognized as a champion.

Bruce Le—one of the more famous Bruce Lee imitators. Bruce has all the talents to become a great kung fu film star. His uncanny resemblance to Bruce Lee has helped his career.

Jacky Chan, the star of *Drunken Master* and *Snake in the Eagle's Shadow*. Jacky is the number one money-maker in the kung fu films today. He has been in films for over a decade. He presently lives in Canada.

Cynthia Rothrock, a kung fu practitioner recognized as the top women's forms competitor in the United States. She has over a decade of teaching and training and is a real credit to the sport. Soon to be a kung fu movie star!

Sifu Kenny Jong, disciple of Shing Yi kung fu. Over thirty years of dedication to the martial arts. Doctor of Chinese medicine and herbalogy.

Dragon Lee, one of the numerous Bruce Lee impersonators. He is very popular in Asia and the United States. A real martial artist and body builder. It was an honor to work with Dragon Lee on *Kung Fu Fever.*

Mr. Sekwii Sha, founder of Shanando style, former New York State champion in sparring, form, and weapons. Over twenty years of training. Former disciple of Grandmaster Urban.

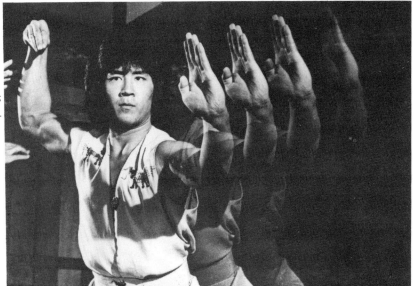

Conan Lee, the star of *Ninja in the Dragon's Den.* A student of the martial arts from childhood. Destined to become a real superstar!

Simon Yuen, a great character actor famous for his roles as the old sifu. Simon has costarred with Jacky Chan in *Drunken Master* and *Snake in the Eagle's Shadow.* A real professional.

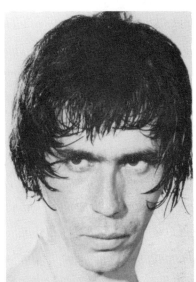

Charles "La Pantera" Bonet—my good friend for over twenty years. Charles is a former U.S. Karate Champion and All Okinawa Weapons and Form champion. We worked together on three films: *The Black Dragon's Revenge, Super Weapon,* and *Way of the Black Dragon.* It has been my honor and a pleasure working with "La Pantera." Charles is a great martial artist and a good friend.

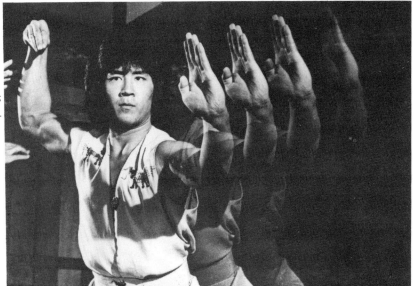

Hwang Jang Lee, one of the best kickers in the movies today. Presently with Seasonal Films. Hwang is always a villain—a great character actor with astounding kicking abilities.

John Liu, one of the best kicker's on the screen. Known for his famous kicking techniques. John lives in Paris. He is the founder of the Zen Do Kwan Association. I was introduced to John by Grandmaster Leung Ting in Hong Kong in the early 1970s.

Kurata—one of my all-time favorites! Kurata is not only a great actor, but an amazing director. He is one of the flashiest fighters on the silver screen. He has more than fifty action films to his credit.

Henry Sanada, one of the greatest new film stars to come from Japan. *Ninja in the Dragon's Den* is a classic kung fu film. Henry's performance was incredible. All of his fighting sequences were choreographed with astounding detail and clarity. It is my opinion that Henry will become world renowned.

Jason Pai Piao was the star of the first film I made in the Philippines. *The Tough Guy* was my film debut in Asia. Jason was very support-ive. He said that I was going to be the best! That was really nice of him. Normally, Orientals keep compliments to themselves. Jason is a good friend and kung fu brother. He is now in a television series in Hong Kong and is very successful.

Fred Giddens. This man really helped me in forming my basics in full-contact sparring. While on location in Korea filming *Kung Fu Fever,* I met Master Giddens. After I felt his left hook on my jaw, we became good friends. Fred has experience in boxing and full-contact sparring. He is an imaginative and creative trainer. Fred is one of the top trainers and former competitors in the United States.

Bill "Superfoot" Wallace has been a multiple world champion. He is known to have the fastest left leg in karate! I have had the pleasure and honor to fight with Bill on several occasions. Our encounters were something special. He is a great karateman and a good friend.

The Reverend Ronald Taganashi. Shihan Taganashi is the founder of the Heaven and Earth Society. He is the foremost authority on ninja technology in the United States. I trained in ninja arts with Shihan Taganashi in the early 1960s into the early 1970s. I will always remember the tremendous workouts that he put me through. He has a gentle spirit with the heart of a lion! Shihan has contributed much to the world of the martial arts in the past three decades.

Master John Kuhl—former Canadian and premier referee! Founder of Combat Karate and trainer to many champions. I met John in the mid-1960s and we became friends.

Chuck Norris. I have known Chuck for about twenty years. He has always been a gentleman and a real champion. He is a member of the Black Belt Hall of Fame. Chuck is a six-time World Champion. After retiring, Chuck became a movie superstar. Chuck has been one of the few real technicians in sport karate. Good luck, Chuck!

Jay T. Will (left) and Joe Lewis (right). Jay T. Will is one of the best referees on the circuit. He is the most visible referee in the world. Jay works for the Professional Karate Association. Joe Lewis was one of the greatest tournament fighters of the 1960s and 1970s. Joe made the transition from noncontact to full contact. Joe Lewis is a real champion—he held the world heavyweight championship longer than anyone in the history of full-contact and noncontact karate.

Grandmasters Frank Ruiz (right) and Pete Siringano, two great pioneers of American martial arts. I studied seven years with Grandmaster Ruiz. It was some of the most outrageous training I have received in the past thirty years. Grandmaster Ruiz is the founder of Nisei Goju, one of the strongest styles created in the early 1960s. He has taught many national and world champions. Ruiz retired undefeated when tournaments were really tournaments. Grandmaster Siringano is one of the best exponents of jujitsu in the United States. He has over four decades of karate-jitsu experience. He has taught many local and international champions. Both of these men are legends in their own time. I learned a great deal from their spirit and courage. These men are the roots of American karate.

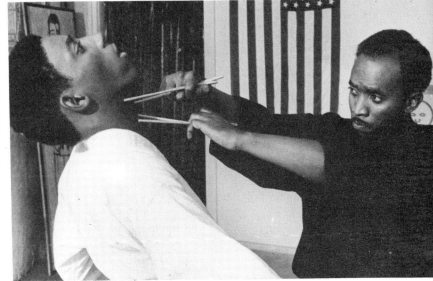

Grandmaster Ronald Duncan has been involved with the martial arts for over three decades. His specialty is ninja arts. He is the foremost authority on ninja technique in the United States. Grandmaster Duncan has demonstrated all over the world. His students have become national and international champions. Grandmaster Duncan has been a credit to the world of the martial arts. I will always feel honored by his presence.

RON VAN CLIEF ATTACK POINT CHART

1. *Cervical Vertebra*. Connects the head to the spinal column. A reverse chop hit to this area could cause permanent damage.
2. *Glabella*. This protects the brain from injury. An iron elbow strike or kick to this area can easily cause unconsciousness.
3. *Mandible*. This is the jawbone. A kick or hook punch to this area would cause a fracture. The uppercut is an excellent technique for this target. The hook kick to the face, jaw or temple will cause a temporary blackout.
4. *Dental foramen*. The chin is a good target for punches and kicking devices. A strike to this area will cause the teeth to shatter from impact. An upward elbow strike to this target.
5. *Humerus bone*. Attaches the arm to the shoulder with the scapula and the clavicle. Any over-extension of this area is caused by a lever or a lock from the aiki system.
6. *Rib cage*. This area is very open to punches and kicks. In combat situations keep your elbows close to your rib cage for protection. A side kick to the ribs is an excellent offensive technique.
7. *Humerus*. This bone connects the arm to the shoulder. The deltoid, bicep and tricep muscles cover this bone.
8. *Rib cage*. The low rib cage is very weak. A front kick or uppercut to this area is most effective. Sometimes a round kick to the stomach will cut the wind and break ribs.
9. *Spinal Column*. The vertebrae are very weak! They should never be contacted by punches and kicks. Paralysis and unconsciousness are the effects of strikes to this area. A strike to the spine can have permanent results!
10. *Elbow joint*. This point is where the humerus connects with the ulna bones. The forearm joins the upper arm in punching actions. Break or dislocate this joint to cause pain and shock. A knee or elbow strike to this target is very effective.
11. *Sacrum*. This area is very suseptible to shock and impact force. A kick or punch to this area can be fatal.
12. *Coccyx*. This is the tip of the spine. A very sensitive area to attack. A throw or sweep can affect this area through shock waves.
13. *Radius and Ulna*. These are the forearm bones. Striking this area causes muscle spasms and contusions. Muscle bruises and separations are easily done with simple blocking and striking mechanisms.
14. *Styloid process*. This joint is very susceptible to injury. It is a very delicate area. Aiki jitsu locks, levers and holds cause intense pain and structural damage.
15. *Femur*. This is the largest bone in the thigh. Kicking the side of the thigh can cause a muscle separation. The round kick to the thigh is most effective!
16. *Patella*. The kneecap should be protected at all times. Constant motion is best. Never be a sitting target. A side kick or hook kick to the kneecap can have crippling effects.
17. *Tibia*. The largest bone in the calf. This bone can be shattered with a side thrust kick to the target. A low front kick to the tibia bone can dislocate the knee joint.
18. *Fibula*. The smallest bone in the calf. A back kick to the knee or fibula can make the suspension system unstable. Side and back kicks work well in combination to the fibula.
19. *Tarsus, Metatarsus and Phalanges* are the major bones of the foot. There are 27 bones in the foot. Stamping downward onto the foot can cause severe pain and injury.
20. *Lateral and medial malleolus* are the bones that connect the shinbone to the ankle joint and the foot. A sweep or kick could cause permanent damage to this area. Twisting the ankle can break the bones of the ankle and foot. Aiki is most effective when attacking this target.

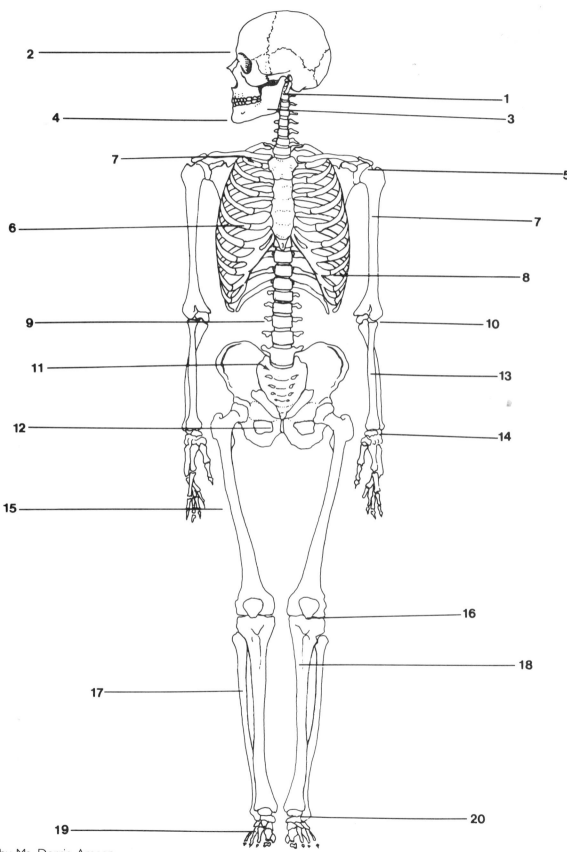

2

1

4   3

7

5

6   7

8

9   10

11   13

12   14

15

16

18

17

19   20

Illustration by Ms. Dorrie Ameen

THE RON VAN CLIEF SYSTEM MUSCLE ACTION GROUP CHART KEY

1. *Deltoid.* Shoulder muscle used in pushing and punching actions. Push-ups and military press stimulate deltoid development. Dips are great!

2. *Pectoralis major.* Chest muscle used in pushing and punching actions. Bench-press or push-up with a medium to wide hand distancing. In punching the arm, shoulder and chest muscles groups combine with the leg muscle groups to amplify hit power!

3. *Triceps.* A large muscle located between the shoulder and the forearm muscles. The rear upper muscle behind the biceps. Push-ups are an excellent exercise to strengthen the triceps. The triceps and forearm muscles increase the muscle action, thus intensifying the hit power.

4. *Forearm group.* Brachialis and brachioradialis are the two largest muscles in the forearm. The forearm group allows the opening and closing of the hand. The action is pushing and pulling. Strong forearm muscles allow for tiger grabbing techniques. The upper and lower muscles of the arm help develop speed and power.

5. *Rectus abdominus.* This group of muscles is developed by sit-ups, jackknives and leg raises. Correct eating habits and a fitness program keep the midsection fit.

6. *Biceps.* This muscle pulls the arm closer to the body. The biceps is basically a pulling muscle used in grabbing and holding. The snake form uses the biceps muscle for chokes and trapping hands. Pull-ups or barbell curls are great for developing the biceps muscle!

7. *Trapezius.* This muscle is used in punching and pulling actions. It runs from the top of the shoulder to the middle of the back. The trapezius is used in punching actions like the hook and uppercut. Barbell shoulder-shrugs and dead lifts develop the trapezius muscle.

8. *Gluteus maximus.* This muscle group helps in kicking mechanisms. Proper rotation of the hip with the leg extension insures powerful kicking techniques. Half squats and deep knee bends are great for this muscle group. Jogging and jumping rope tone up this area.

9. *Rectus femoris.* Sometimes called the front thigh biceps. This is the primary muscle used in extending the leg. Therefore, it is of utmost importance to develop this area. Leg extensions and deep knee bends are excellent for this area.

10. *Gastrocnemius.* Sometimes called the calf muscle. This muscle is used in the various kicking actions. Good calf muscles help to strengthen your forward explosive action. The calf muscle allows good push-off action of the legs. Jumping rope, jogging, aerobic exercise and progressive resistance effectively develop this muscle.

11. *External oblique.* This muscle group is used in twisting and turning actions necessary in punching and kicking mechanisms. Pushing and pulling drills tone this area. Continuous kicking techniques keep this area fit!

12. *Latissimus dorsi.* Sometimes referred to as the "lats." This muscle is used in pushing and pulling actions used in punching actions. Lats pull-downs or rowing motions tone the upper back.

13. *Biceps femoris.* Sometimes called the rear thigh biceps. This muscle is used to pull the leg back toward the body. The rear thigh biceps pulls the hook, side, round, and back kick back to the chamber. This muscle retracts the leg. Leg curls, bike riding, rope jumping and multiple kicking drills tone this muscle.

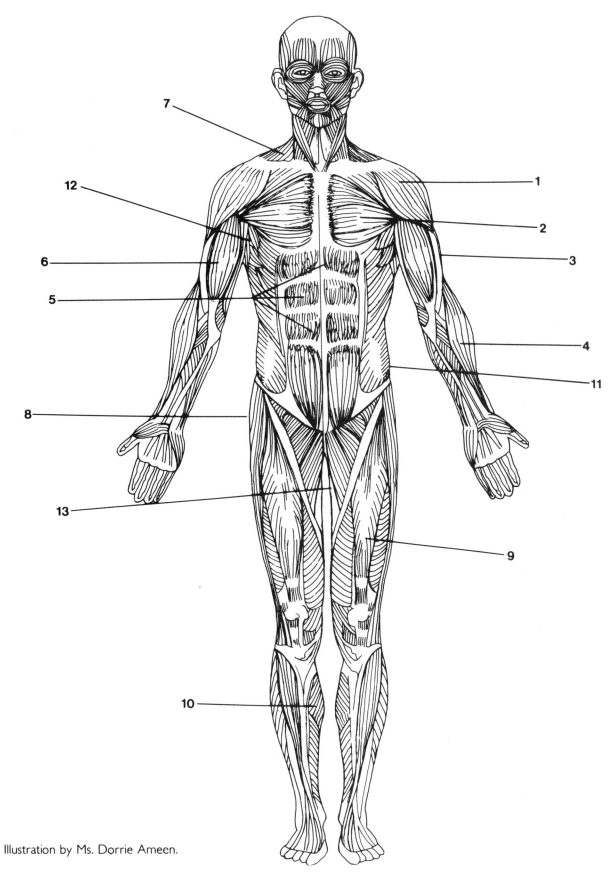

Illustration by Ms. Dorrie Ameen.

INDEX